MAJOR TAX REFORM: URGENT NECESSITY OR NOT?

Second in the seventh series of Rational Debate Seminars
sponsored by the American Enterprise Institute
held at
American Enterprise Institute
Washington, D. C.

ROBERT GORALSKI
Moderator

MAJOR TAX REFORM: URGENT NECESSITY OR NOT?

Charls E. Walker
Henry S. Reuss

RATIONAL DEBATE SERIES

American Enterprise Institute for Public Policy Research
Washington, D. C.

FOREWORD

"No taxation without representation!" was a rallying cry of the American Revolution. In the two centuries since, tax reform has been a recurring preoccupation of represented and representative alike.

This book presents the views on taxation and tax reform of two well-known experts, Representative Henry S. Reuss of Wisconsin and former Under Secretary of the Treasury Charls E. Walker. The discussion took place on the evening of 21 February 1973 as the twenty-fifth in AEI's series of televised Rational Debates.

The participants addressed themselves to such questions as: Who *really* pays taxes? Do those in the upper income brackets carry their "fair share" of the tax burden? Should more of the tax load be shifted to corporations? Is the American tax system biased in favor of consumption or savings and investment? Are there "loopholes," and if so, why and what are their effects?

Debate and the competition of ideas is fundamental to public policy formulation in a free society. Such reasoned jousting is especially important in the field of tax policy, for any change may have far-reaching economic and social consequences. It is hoped that the contrasting ideas and proposals set forth here will contribute to wise public policy choices.

August 1973

William J. Baroody
President
American Enterprise Institute
for Public Policy Research

CONTENTS

FIRST LECTURE

Federal Income Taxation — Myths and Realities

CHARLS E. WALKER

It is distressing to witness growing confusion over the federal income tax system. The American people and the American taxpayer deserve better. They need to be informed, not misled—enlightened, not confused.

Discussions and debate over taxes—their level, equity and even morality—have been going on throughout recorded history. Some developed into revolutions or wars. So perhaps we should not be surprised that the subject is forever with us and frequently generates more heat than light.

The main problem is that everyone has his or her own strongly held and emotional views on tax matters. The views here in the United States are usually expressed in regular sequence. Around April 15 of each year, when millions of Americans fill out their returns, there is intensive discussion of taxes. In addition to the seasonal peak, there is another time when tax discussions may become very emotional. That is in the summer and early fall of years divisible by four. Some of the rhetoric about taxes that surfaced during the 1972 campaign is still being repeated and should be laid to rest once and for all.

Four years ago I would have stoutly resisted the role that I am playing tonight—that is, trying to separate fact from fiction, myth from reality, in the current public discussions of the federal tax system. But during my four years in the

Treasury Department, I helped steer through Congress two major tax bills—the Tax Reform Act of 1969 and the Revenue Act of 1971. In the process, I began to feel about taxes a little like the boy who had to read a book about penguins. He concluded that he learned more about penguins than he really wanted to know.

The subject of taxes causes emotional responses because nobody likes to pay them. But as Justice Oliver Wendell Holmes so aptly stated: "Taxes are what we pay for a civilized society." Justice Holmes, as usual, was correct. The primary purpose of taxes is to raise the revenues to pay the cost of governing this great nation.

This fundamental purpose raises the first in a series of debatable points. How big should the public sector of our economy be? Obviously, the more government spends, the more it will have to raise in revenues to pay the bills. As people demand more government services and programs, they should at the same time know that they are also increasing the pressure to increase taxes.

Debate on this particular issue—the size of government —is now in full swing. The Nixon administration believes the best way to prevent a need for increased taxes is to tighten up on federal spending. Others believe that taxes should be increased to pay for additional government programs and activities. Unfortunately, under our system we are often asked to take our choice *before* we pay our money. Spending programs are frequently established before we get the tab.

In addition to raising revenues, many other considerations must enter into tax policy. We want our system to be efficient, simple, and equitable; we also want it to work so as to further, rather than impede, the achievement of our social and economic goals.

Take first the matter of simplicity. It would be simple indeed to have everyone pay in taxes the same percentage on all income across the board. Just pick a figure and apply it to all people and all income. This approach might meet the test of simplicity, but it would ignore other highly important considerations.

The first cries would be that the system violated the principle of progressivity. People in higher income brackets would not pay a higher percentage of income in taxes than those who are not so well off.

But other loud screams would be heard from those who insist on equity. The American people, time after time, have supported what they consider to be fair and equitable income tax deductions. For example, the vast majority of Americans think it is only fair that a family that is hit with major medical expenses be allowed to deduct part of that expense in figuring income taxes. Support for this provision of the tax code is so strong that it was never seriously questioned in the deliberations on the Tax Reform Act of 1969.

Over the years, efforts to meet the test of fairness have made the tax laws much more complicated. For example, the average taxpayer may have trouble figuring out the provisions covering noninsured casualty losses. They seem very complicated—and they are. But many homeowners who were unfortunate enough to be hit by tropical storm Agnes last summer would rather put up with the complexity than suffer the loss of home and property without some relief from income taxes.

As deductions have expanded to cover specific situations, individuals form definite opinions. Just ask any taxpayer. A deduction is anything that he is legally entitled to. A loophole is a deduction that applies to someone else.

The tax system should also be used to meet certain social goals. A good example was the provision in the 1969 legislation allowing a faster write-off or depreciation of antipollution equipment for business. Another provision encouraged the rehabilitation of slum housing. Still another example is the long-standing provision for the deduction of contributions to church and charity.

A fourth main criteria involves the use of our tax system to promote economic goals. Economic growth requires a strong and continuous flow of productive investment. When we talk about employment, for example, it is fundamental to understand that it takes on the average an investment of $30,000 to support one job in manufacturing. In terms of economic growth, it is also imperative to consider the impact of tax policy on our international competitive position.

In short, our tax policies must take into account simplicity and equity and should promote our social and economic objectives.

Now let me discuss some myths that have gained currency in the past few months.

MYTH: Rich people get away with murder when it comes to paying federal income taxes.

REALITY: This myth seems to have grown out of the disclosure some months ago of some highly misleading and incomplete data indicating that over 100 individuals with more than $200,000 in adjusted gross income paid no federal income taxes in 1970.

The first point to note is that the returns from which this information was drawn were unaudited. As the audit process has taken place, the number of nontaxpayers has dropped sharply and now stands at only eighty-five. This number will undoubtedly decline further as the audits continue and as certain "staged-in" provisions of the Tax Reform Act of 1969 become fully effective.

It is also important to note that even the figure of eighty-five high-income individuals who pay no federal income taxes compares most favorably with the more than 300 reported in the mid-1960s.

Stated differently, the Tax Reform Act signed by President Nixon in December 1969—the most massive revision of the Internal Revenue Code in history—*is* proving to be highly effective in reducing the number of rich people who pay no income taxes. But I would not be surprised if, from reading the papers lately, you had received the opposite impression.

Moreover, so much attention has been paid to this handful of nontaxpayers that those with incomes above $200,000 who do pay big taxes have been almost wholly overlooked. In contrast to the eighty-five or less who paid no taxes, more than 15,200 (or 99 percent-plus) did, and they paid heavily —an average of $177,000 per person for a total of $2.7 billion. This is an effective rate of 44 percent on adjusted gross income and 60 percent on taxable income.

Rich people do pay taxes, and those who claim otherwise are either ignorant of the facts or deliberately ignore the facts.

MYTH: The Tax Reform Act of 1969 greatly increased the complexity for the typical taxpayer of preparing and filing his return.

REALITY: The 1969 act made taxpaying much simpler for 25 million taxpayers (about one-third of the total).

Through enactment of President Nixon's low-income allowance, some 12 million low-income individuals (poverty level or below) were removed completely from the tax rolls —and you cannot make taxpaying any simpler than that. In addition, the 1969 law made it attractive for another 13 million taxpayers to use the standard deduction and thus avoid the time and trouble of itemizing their deductions.

The 1969 act did make taxpaying more complicated for one type of individual—the one in several thousand who finds it advantageous to hire an expert lawyer or accountant to devise investment shelters that minimize his federal income tax. There is absolutely nothing illegal about this. But the 1969 act did take an important step toward tax equity by enacting for the first time a minimum income tax aimed at collecting some amount of taxes from all citizens with high incomes.

The sharp reduction in the number of high-income people paying no federal taxes indicates that the minimum income tax—along with other tax-tightening provisions of the 1969 act—have been at least partially successful in this respect.

It is, of course, too early to say how successful. We need more information before we go further.

MYTH: The Tax Reform Act of 1969 and the Revenue Act of 1971 provided a "bonanza" to business and the rich while increasing taxes on the working man.

REALITY: For the four years 1969 through 1972, these two acts (including the new administrative guidelines permitting accelerated depreciation of new business equipment) raised the tax bill on corporations by $5 billion, but lowered the bill for individuals (mainly low- and middle-income) by almost $19 billion. And this latter figure does not include the $3½ billion tax cut from repeal of the excise tax on automobiles—a benefit accruing mostly to individuals.

As to rich individuals versus those not so well off, the President's low-income allowance, as already noted, removed all persons at or below the poverty level from the tax rolls. Beyond this, individuals paying taxes in the bottom bracket had their tax bills reduced by 82 percent. Moving on up the income scale, the amount of tax reduction decreased progressively, except in the highest brackets. Individuals with incomes of over $100,000 actually had their tax payments increased by 7½ percent.

Again, I would not be surprised if you had received just the opposite impression from statements made in recent discussions of taxes.

MYTH: By raising taxes on corporations, the government can avoid raising them on individuals.

REALITY: This myth is one of the most deeply rooted of all.

In the final analysis, corporations do not pay taxes—people do. The corporation is simply a legal arrangement for doing business—an arrangement which, incidentally, has proved highly efficient in helping to meet the ever-growing economic needs of man. To determine which persons the corporate tax really hits, several questions have to be considered.

Is the corporation in a strong enough market position to pass on the tax to its customers? If so, the corporate income tax hits the individual something like a sales tax, and if the tax is on a business that produces necessities, its impact may be regressive—hitting poor people relatively harder than rich people.

If the corporation cannot pass on the tax, then it must be absorbed by the owners (stockholders) in the form of lower profits and dividends. Still, however, it is people who bear the tax. Many of these people have high incomes, but as already noted, the 1969 act increased the tax burden on the very rich by $7\frac{1}{2}$ percent. It should also be noted that some 30 million taxpayers directly own, and an additional 70 million indirectly own, stock in corporations.

In the long run, a corporation, if it is to remain a going concern, clearly must pass on all of its taxes in one way or another. But in the short run, economists—although in disagreement—appear to believe that about half of the corporate profits tax is passed on to customers and about half is borne by stockholders. This is why some European countries are moving toward an income tax credit to corporate shareholders in order to reduce the double taxation on corporate dividends.

The question of whom the corporate tax hits is difficult to answer—except that it does not, as some would have you believe, fall only on "big business." In one way or another, taxes are always paid by the people.

MYTH: The job development investment credit and the easing of depreciation guidelines in the 1971 tax act were giveaways to business that fail to help the working man.

REALITY: Economists of all persuasions have recognized for many years that productive investment is the mainspring in creating new jobs, raising the standard of living of the working man, and maintaining and sharpening U.S. competitiveness in world markets. President Kennedy recognized this in 1961 and 1962 when he eased depreciation guidelines and proposed the first tax credit for investment in new equipment.

In 1971, this nation incurred its first trade deficit in the twentieth century and the deficit more than doubled in 1972. Our competitiveness abroad had become severely eroded. Rather than criticizing investment-spurring changes in the tax laws as giveaways, the critics of these actions would do well to ponder what made this country so richly productive in the first place, and where we will stand in the international trading race in the future if their advice is heeded.

MYTH: We occasionally hear that this or that section of the tax code was enacted by mistake—that Congress did not thoroughly consider it.

REALITY: This might be the biggest myth of all. The House Ways and Means Committee—which originates all tax legislation—is one of the hardest working committees in Congress. It has a staff of top professionals. The members themselves are intimately familiar with the tax laws, and they hold extensive hearings on tax matters. Having worked closely with both the Ways and Means Committee and the Senate Finance Committee on many bills, I can guarantee that changes are not made accidentally in the tax code.

This list of myths and realities concerning the federal income tax system is by no means exhaustive; I could list several more. But I think I have covered enough to illustrate my point—many of the recent discussions about taxes have generated much rhetoric and little substance.

Let me conclude with three observations.

First, our federal income tax system is not perfect, but it is basically fair and effective—and, as a result of the Tax Reform Act of 1969 and the Revenue Act of 1971, it is a much better system than we had only four years ago.

As noted earlier, people with high incomes *do* pay taxes, and heavily. Marginal rates range up to 70 percent on so-called "unearned income" and to 50 percent on "earned income." When all the various preferences are accounted for, effective rates range from about 10 percent to upwards of 30 percent. This range of progressivity would undoubtedly not satisfy those who believe that all high-income individuals are crooks and who therefore insist on "soaking the rich." But I submit that it is an acceptable range to most fair-minded people.

Nor would an impartial observer conclude that all of the preferences which combine to scale down the effective rate serve no national purpose and therefore should be expunged from the law. Each preference should be evaluated in terms of the purpose it serves. Such evaluation should not be made in the context of rich versus poor people, corporations versus individuals, et cetera, but in terms of a careful and unemotional review of its history and effectiveness.

Recent discussions of taxes might lead the uninformed observer to conclude that this is never done. Quite the contrary, the House Ways and Means Committee and the Senate Finance Committee went over the Internal Revenue Code with a fine-toothed comb in 1969 and are expected to repeat that effort in this Congress. The results will not satisfy those critics who aver that the income tax system is riddled with unfair provisions (which it is not), but I am confident that the people's representatives will continue the hard but relatively thankless work of improving the tax laws.

Second, the real issue in the tax arena now is the level of taxes that the typical American bears and what he gets for his money in the form of government services. In state after state, county after county, and precinct after precinct, taxpayers are asking whether the money they send to Washington is being used efficiently and effectively in solving national problems. And in many instances the answer is "no."

This is why last summer's tax reform issue has been transformed into the battle of the budget—as more and more people have concluded that the power to spend is in reality the power to tax.

The American people may benefit in two ways from this battle. The centering of attention on the task of bringing federal spending under control may permit the tax committees to reexamine the Internal Revenue Code in a systematic manner, without being forced to the excesses that unin-

11

formed public opinion can sometimes produce. More importantly, public dissatisfaction with the level and form of federal spending may well result in effective action by Congress to put its fiscal house in order. If so, the tax reform discussion, however uninformed and misleading, will have been worthwhile.

Third and finally, I seriously doubt that those congressmen and others who are preoccupied with so-called loophole closing are really asking the right questions about our income tax system. This does not mean that sincere efforts to make the tax system equitable—within the constraints of providing deliberate inequities in order to promote proper economic and social goals—should not be made. But the public should not be led to expect big changes or—and here is where many politicians are culpable—sufficient "loophole-closing" to permit a significant cut in the tax bill of the typical American. (Does not "tax reform" mean to the typical voter—reform taxes so you can cut mine, and above all don't spend the proceeds to support an ever-growing federal establishment?)

The public interest would be much better served if the following query were put and debated: Is our tax system, as now constituted, the fundamental system that we need to serve our basic economic and social goals in the remainder of this century? I happen to think the answer is no—but *not* because of the so-called loopholes.

Our tax system is deficient absolutely and relative to those in other advanced industrial nations because it falls much too heavily on savings and investment; in other words, it is biased in favor of consumption. This results partly from our reliance on taxes on income instead of taxes on spending. It also reflects our relatively heavier taxation of business enterprise and capital gains.

Rather than preoccupying ourselves with loopholes, we should instead be debating the merits and demerits of a consumption-based value-added tax—a system that will become uniform among members of the European Economic Community. Can such a tax be made nonregressive, as its supporters maintain? If so, it could well have much to commend it, since it is a tax on spending rather than income, and therefore does not contain the built-in bias against savings and investment that is inherent in an income tax.

For example, under our present tax system, if you and I both have the same income, deductions and credits, our income tax liability will be the same—even though you are thrifty and support the saving-investment process directly or through financial intermediaries, and I may blow my funds on frivolous consumption. But under a consumption-based (investment goods exempted) value-added tax, my tax liability would be greater than yours, because my spending on consumption would be greater than yours. In effect, the tax system would reward you for supporting the savings and investment that is the mainspring of economic growth in an advanced industrial nation.

One of the most ignored aspects of our federal tax system relates to our increasing reliance on payroll taxes. Such taxes begin with the first dollar of a worker's income and therefore are highly regressive. Here again, a system of value-added taxes deserves serious consideration, since all or a portion of the revenue so raised could and probably should be used to reduce the regressivity of payroll taxes.

These concluding comments only scratch the surface of the tax discussion that should be taking place, but, unfortunately, is not. Perhaps the American Enterprise Institute can, through future debates, direct informed discussion toward these knotty but most important issues.

SECOND LECTURE

The Need for Tax Reform

HENRY S. REUSS

"To tax and to please, no more than to love and be wise, is given to no man." No tax is popular, and no taxpayer feels that others are paying their fair share.

American history is marked by surges of popular feeling against the "unfairness" of all kinds of taxes. An excise tax on grain produced the Whiskey Rebellion of the eighteenth century. High protective tariffs helped cause the Populist movement late in the nineteenth century. And various inequities of the federal income tax have led to the "taxpayers' revolt" of recent years. As Edmund Burke knew, taxes are a very tangible price to pay for government services which often appear intangible to the taxpayer, and thus are an obvious target of discontent.

Tax reform is not the unique prerogative of modern day populism, however. There are economic reasons for tax reform every bit as compelling as considerations of equity. Many a large corporation and wealthy individual have as much to gain from a sane and efficient tax system as the hard-pressed, modest-income taxpayer.

Four questions must be raised in evaluating the federal income tax system, of which "fairness" is only one:

1. Does it raise enough revenues?
2. Does it encourage full employment and economic prosperity in the United States?
3. Does it interfere with economic efficiency?

4. Is it fair?

Our federal income tax structure meets none of these criteria. Eroded by unjustifiable preferences, it is fiscally inadequate, job-threatening, economically inefficient, and socially inequitable. It stands in need of thorough reform.

1. Tax Reform to Raise Additional Revenue

My first criticism of our present tax system is that it just does not raise enough revenue.

For years, the United States has counted on a fiscal dividend in peacetime—the surplus of revenues over expenditures generated by an expanding gross national product (GNP)—to fund new programs and to permit tax reductions. Today, we have peace of a sort—but no fiscal dividend. What happened to it?

What happened is that the rate of increase of civilian expenditures outstripped that of GNP, and that the rate of increase of federal income tax revenues lagged behind that of GNP. Civilian expenditures increased at an annual rate of only 6 percent from 1960 to 1965. Thereafter, due in large part to climbing social security outlays and new domestic legislation, the annual rate of increase accelerated to 9.1 percent from 1965 to 1970 and to 10.3 percent from 1970 to 1973. Civilian expenditures claimed only 8.8 percent of GNP in 1965 but that share had jumped to 14.5 percent by 1973.

At the same time, federal income taxes were falling as a percentage of GNP. In 1963, the income tax on individuals and corporations yielded an amount equivalent to 12.7 percent of GNP. In 1973, three tax cuts later (1964, 1969, and 1971), the income tax yield was some $45 billion less than it would have been under 1963 laws, and amounted to only 11 percent of GNP.[1]

Since 1965, the federal budget has been in surplus only once. Particularly spectacular deficits were shown in 1971, 1972, and 1973, despite reduced national defense real costs.

Two disquieting recent studies have predicted that the budget squeeze will continue almost throughout the 1970s. Exploding the myth of a post-Vietnam peace dividend, the 1972 Brookings Institution report entitled *Setting National Priorities* estimated, assuming continued program trends, that full-employment expenditures would outrun full-employment revenues "substantially" through 1975 and that revenues would not exceed expenditures until at least 1977, when such excess would be "a very modest amount."[2] An American Enterprise Institute study reached similar conclusions, although based on slightly different assumptions: not until 1978 "would there be substantial room in the budget for new programs without either reducing ongoing programs or initiatives or raising taxes."[3]

The 1974 federal budget validates these projections. Faced with a self-imposed trio of unpopular possibilities—courting inflation via another huge deficit, asking for a general tax increase, or cutting programs—President Nixon chose the third, and least unpopular, course.

I applaud the President for cutting back outmoded and ineffective programs where he has done so. As I said to Office of Management and Budget Director Roy Ash on February 8, any budget director who has the foresight to end appropriations for the worthless Subversive Activities Control Board cannot be all bad! The so-called "impacted" school aid program benefitting such wealthy areas as nearby Montgomery County, Maryland, was another excellent candidate for evisceration. So was the antiballistic missile site for the Washington area.

All of his proposed cuts will not, of course, be enacted, nor do they deserve to be. The federal government has assumed wide responsibilities in the last thirty-five years. I do not believe that Americans are suddenly going to resign themselves to filthy air and water, neglected poor and aged, and illiterate minority children.

In short, my sense of social values tells me that the American people, and the Congress, will not long be content with the pinched level of spending postulated for the fiscal 1974 and succeeding budgets. That is not to say, I emphasize, that Congress should go off on an orgy of uncontrolled deficit spending in order to fund these desired domestic programs. On the contrary, as a member of the special Joint Study Committee on Budget Control, I am now attempting to work out a congressional budget procedure which will compel the Congress to assert control over both income and outgo.

If Americans want the expenditures on the great priorities of national need which I believe they do, the Congress will have to find additional revenues. To attempt to secure those revenues today from a general tax increase would be politically difficult and economically deflationary. Thus all, or a large part, of the needed additional revenues must come from tax reform—plugging tax loopholes—from money which goes not primarily for consumption or useful investment, but instead goes largely for bidding up the price of stocks, commodities, and real estate, or into foreign adventures.

In the 1974 budget, $5 billion is cut from Department of Health, Education, and Welfare programs benefitting primarily the old, the poor, and the disadvantaged, while the same amount is transferred via the asset depreciation range system and the investment tax credit to corporations and wealthy investors. The emergency employment assistance program is phased out, to save $670 million, while a tax break worth three times that amount permits wealthy persons to pass on appreciated property to their heirs at death without paying a capital gains tax. The American public, I assert, is quite ready to reverse these priorities.

Even without invoking these needed social expenditures as a reason for revenue-raising tax reform, it is apparent that the Nixon 1974 budget itself is going to run out of revenues. After a $17 billion cut mainly in domestic programs, the 1974 budget has only the narrowest full-employment surplus: $.3 billion, less even than the original projected 1973 full-employment surplus of $.7 billion, which has now been revised to an estimated deficit of $2.4 billion. And the budget gives a bleak picture for the next few years: "The projected budget margins for 1975-78 are relatively small and quite precarious." [4]

These precarious budget margins will crumble shortly when Mr. Nixon comes up with several promised programs —billions for relief and reconstruction in both North and South Vietnam and tax relief for the hard-pressed American property taxpayer. It is not realistic to look to further expenditure cuts to accommodate these additional billions. Therefore, unless Mr. Nixon wishes to impose a general tax increase, or to feed the fires of inflation with uncontrolled budget deficits, he himself could use the additional revenues that come from judicious loophole-plugging!

The solution, I repeat, is not to trigger a new round of inflation through a badly calculated full-employment deficit. Nor do we require a general tax increase. The only sensible approach is to repair the revenue erosion of the last ten years by plugging tax loopholes.

How much revenue could be raised by ending all tax preferences? Estimates range from the Department of the Treasury's 1971 figure of $36 billion to Pechman and Okner's 1972 figure of $77 billion.[5] Former Assistant Secretary of the Treasury Stanley S. Surrey put the figure at $50—$60 billion in his recent testimony before the House Ways and Means Committee.[6] Smaller, and thus politically more realistic, amounts could be obtained from a number of bills currently before the 93rd Congress. H.R. 1040, introduced by Representative James C. Corman with forty-three cosponsors, would raise $20 billion by plugging loopholes in some eighteen areas. Senator Muskie's proposed bill would find $18.6 billion annually by concentrating on twenty-four loopholes. My own H.R. 967, with fifty-seven cosponsors, would obtain a "quick yield" of $9 billion by closing wholly or in part eight loopholes—special treatment for capital gains (the alternate rate, the six-month holding period and the 30 percent corporate maximum rate), capital gains at death, the asset depreciation range (ADR) system, tax deferral on foreign earnings of U.S. subsidiaries, oil industry preferences, excess farm loss deductions, tax exemption of interest on state and local bonds, and the minimum tax on preference income.

I shall return later to the question of which tax loopholes should be plugged. For the moment, I conclude that tax reform is necessary to avoid painful budget-cutting now and a general tax increase in the near future. Moreover, should a general tax increase become unavoidable later, tax reform would have provided a broadened tax base on which to raise the rates and thus would lessen the per capita additional burden.

2. Tax Reform to Achieve Full Employment and Economic Prosperity

The tax system's primary goal is to raise adequate revenues as fairly as possible. A secondary goal is to further full employment, full utilization of productive capacity, and adequate purchasing power.

The battle for full employment is far from being won. While overall unemployment rates have at last declined from close to 6 percent where they hovered for two years, the 5 percent figure of January 1973 is still unsatisfactory. With 5 percent unemployment, the economy is running at a GNP of some 3 percent—or $38 billion—less than what it would at full employment. This entails a revenue sacrifice of around $12 billion annually.

Furthermore, current unemployment falls unduly on the young and the minorities. In January, 14.3 percent of young people (workers of both sexes, ages 16 to 19) were unemployed. Similarly, 8.9 percent of nonwhites were unable to find work.

Jobs are lost through tax loopholes. Here are some examples:

Taxes on earnings of U.S. subsidiaries abroad. The deferral of U.S. income tax on foreign earnings, which costs U.S. taxpayers at least $250 million a year, encourages corporations to transfer production abroad.

A foreign subsidiary of a U.S. corporation pays the 48 percent U.S. corporate income tax only on that portion of its income which is repatriated to the United States. Thus a U.S. plant is tempted to close down and transfer itself overseas. On goods made in the U.S. plant, the corporation pays a 48 percent federal corporate income tax whether the profits are paid out in dividends or retained. But profits made by an overseas subsidiary are exempt from the U.S. tax as long as they remain overseas —which they often do—where they are either kept in the bank or reinvested.

The Western Hemisphere Trade Corporation deduction similarly encourages corporations to export potential U.S. jobs to Canada, Mexico, and Latin America. The Treasury pays corporations an estimated $115 million a year to do this.[7]

Another gimmick in the tax laws allows a U.S. corporation to get a credit on its federal income tax for a foreign income tax paid. Thus a company with a Wisconsin plant must pay an 11 percent Wisconsin corporate income tax, in addition to the federal income tax, and can only *deduct* the Wisconsin tax, which means that the taxpaying corporation gets less than a 50 percent benefit from deducting the Wisconsin corporate income tax. If the tax at a similar rate—11 percent in our example—is paid a foreign country, however, the foreign tax is *credited,* and thus is worth about twice as much to the corporate taxpayer. This constitutes still another tax incentive to locate abroad rather than at home.

With these three tax disincentives, American corporations have abundant reason to locate abroad. The threat of losing American jobs by excessive multinational investment overseas is already a very real one because foreign wage rates are frequently only a fraction of American wage rates. Adding on a perverse tax incentive to leave home simply adds insult to injury. And ironically, it is the American worker who has to make up by his own taxes that which multinational corporations avoid paying —$2 to $3 billion a year—by reason of these loopholes. So it is the American worker who has had to pay for fracturing his own job.

The asset depreciation range system and the investment tax credit. Although these tax preferences were sold to Congress as job-makers, they too deserve a close look.

It is true that by subsidizing business investment (though it will tend to be more marginal and less productive than the plant and equipment that would have been created but for the inducement), some jobs are created. Men are put to work building the induced plant and equipment. After several years of force-feeding, however, the existence of all this new capacity is likely to chill later investment and force job cutbacks. The 1973 *Economic Report of the President* put last year's increase in fixed investment at 14 percent; a similar increase is predicted for 1973—the sharpest back-to-back increase since the mid-1960s, when only the buildup of the Vietnam War prevented severe reduction in employment.[8] Furthermore, not only will the rate of investment cost jobs, but the nature of the induced investment itself will mean fewer jobs for American workers. In many instances, manpower will be replaced by labor-saving machinery. Rather than stimulate a frenzy of uneconomic investment through tax breaks, we should aim for a slow and maintained increase in investment.

Our increasingly less progressive tax system should cause us concern about prosperity in an additional important way. Recent data suggest that for the first time in many years, the distribution of income among income groups in America is becoming more unequal.

Starting with the New Deal, the income shares of various segments of American society improved steadily. While the rich got a little richer, the poor, and particularly the fellow in the middle, greatly improved their relative positions. This trend, a result of progressive tax policies and anti-depression programs, continued from mid-century right down through 1968. Comparing income shares of the five fifths of American families, 1950 versus 1968, we find that the lowest fifth's share of total income increased from 4.5 percent to 5.7 percent, the next lowest from 12 to 12.4 percent, the third fifth from 17.4 percent to 17.7 percent, and the fourth fifth from 23.5 to 23.7 percent. Only the share of the top fifth declined, from 42.6 percent to 40.6 percent. The two percentage points that were lopped off the highest fifth were distributed among the lower four fifths—with the greatest gain, properly enough, for the lowest fifth.

Then, after 1968, unemployment almost doubled. Further reductions were made in the progressive income tax at a time when regressive federal payroll, local property, and state sales taxes were rapidly increasing. The income shares for 1971 (the most recent Census Bureau figures available) are as follows, listed in order from the lowest to the highest fifth: 5.5 percent, 11.9 percent, 17.4 percent, 23.7 percent, and 41.6 percent. The top fifth gained a percentage point over 1968 in its total share, the second fifth came out even, and the bottom three fifths went down, with the family in the middle hurt the worst.

Furthermore, while the income share of the richest 5 percent of American families declined from 17.0 percent in 1950 to 14.0 percent in 1968, that figure, too, has risen sharply since 1968. The present percentage is 16.2 percent! [9]

What are we to make of this apparent increasing inequality of income distribution, and the inability of the tax system to correct it? Karl Marx in *Das Kapital* predicted that the final collapse of capitalism would occur when decreasing purchasing power became insufficient to take the goods off the market. This would lead, he wrote, to over-investment and to suicidal competition for a declining market among capitalists themselves. [10]

One does not need to advocate that the tax system be used to bring about absolute equality of income distribution.

In a free market economy, some inequality is necessary to provide capital for investment and incentives to work. But as Karl Marx pointed out, a trend towards increasing inequality is dangerous. A healthy, expanding economy requires broadly based purchasing power. A progressive tax system is an important means of broadening that base. So tax reform, I suggest, may also be necessary to disprove Marx's gloomy prediction.

3. Tax Reform to Achieve Economic Efficiency

Not only does the existing tax system fail to raise adequate revenue. Not only does it erode American jobs and purchasing power. It is also economically inefficient.

There are two ways of looking at the efficiency of taxes. First, to the extent that the government interferes in the private sector through selective tax provisions, do the provisions channel resources where they are most needed? Second, does the tax system achieve its objectives at minimal cost? By either standard, the performance of our present system must be judged poor.

The tax system encourages some forms of investment over others—for example, investment in oil exploration, real estate, capital equipment, and timber—and reduces the amount of capital available for other investment—research and development, high-technology investment, mass transit, new energy sources, and so on.

Here are two examples of inefficient allocation of resources produced by the tax system:

28

Capital gains at death. Capital gain is taxed if the owner of appreciated property sells it, or if he gives it away, during his lifetime. If the owner can hang on to the property until death, no capital gains tax will ever be levied on the amount of appreciation occurring during his life. Thus invested capital tends to get locked into stagnant industries rather than moving into newer, technologically more advanced areas where before-tax profitability might be greater.

Excess farm loss deduction against nonfarm income. It is a curious fact, as the Treasury Department pointed out in 1968 and as the 1970 Treasury figures substantiate, that people with adjusted gross incomes over $50,000 seem incapable of making a profit out of farming. Tax returns for the $2,000 to $3,000 bracket show net farm profits outweighing net farm losses three-to-two. In the $50,000 to $100,000 bracket, profits equal losses. From $100,000 up, losses outweigh profits. Finally, for those with incomes of $1,000,000 or more, losses outweigh profits twenty-to-one.[11]

The pattern for nonfarm business and professional income is completely different.

The tax system thus encourages high-bracket nonfarmers to take advantage of generous farm accounting provisions to write off farm "losses" (actually often only normal capital expenses prematurely written off) against highly taxed nonfarm income. This ties up capital in farming regardless of economic profitability. It also places real farmers at a disadvantage: when they go to buy land, the prices have been bid up; when they go to market, they are undercut by the "hobby farmers."

What are the costs of these tax-induced misallocations of resources, or, for that matter, of tax-induced justifiable allocations? The costs are plenty:

Tax-exempt status of the interest from state and local bonds. This provision of the tax code has a laudable objective—to help state and local governments borrow cheaply. But exempting the interest on municipal bonds from taxation costs the federal government at least *three* dollars in lost revenue from wealthy taxpayers for every *two* dollars channelled to local governments.

Oil industry preferences. The goal of these preferences (the depletion allowance and the option to deduct as a current expense certain intangible exploration and development costs) is to encourage production from domestic petroleum reserves. In 1969, a Treasury Department study concluded that these preferences were grossly inefficient: $1.4 billion in foregone federal revenues stimulated only an additional $140 million in domestic oil reserves a year.[12]

Two reasons for this poor showing seem clear. First, the preferences go indiscriminately to large corporations and to small "wildcatters." (In fact, there is even a tendency for small corporations to run up against the net income limitation more often than large corporations; thus the depletion preference, in particular, may actually give a greater advantage to large corporations than to small ones.) Insofar as the preferences are intended to compensate for risk, it is clearly inefficient to compensate those with less risk (large corporations) at the same rate as those with greater risk (smaller corporations). Significantly, barrels per day crude oil production of smaller oil companies remained almost unchanged between 1961 and 1971 while that of the largest companies (the "Chase Bank group") increased by 50 percent. The Chase group's share of total domestic production of crude oil rose from 63 percent in 1961 to 71 percent in 1971.[13] Thus tax preferences are not uniformly encouraging increased production but instead are fostering concentration within the industry.

Second, and even more senseless, the preferences apply equally to domestic U.S. oil production and to the production of U.S. corporations overseas. In 1960, the most recent year for which figures are available, 23 percent of all depletion was claimed on foreign properties. Since risk and overhead costs are lower abroad, this provision, combined with the foreign tax credit, is an obvious *disincentive* to domestic production.

4. Tax Reform is Necessary for Equity in the Tax System

No tax system, however efficient, is acceptable unless it is fair. Understandably, it is the *unfairness* of the present system—not its economic distortions or inefficiency—which has aroused the deep public reaction known as the "taxpayers' revolt." If I have left this aspect of tax reform to the end, it is not because it is the least important, but because it is more difficult to discuss equity objectively than the need for revenues, jobs, and economic efficiency.

31

Horizontal equity requires that taxpayers with equal incomes (from whatever source) and equal financial responsibilities be taxed the same amount. Vertical equity, under a progressive tax, demands that people with larger incomes pay not only a larger dollar amount in tax but also a greater percent of their income. Our tax system satisfies the requirements of neither horizontal nor vertical equity.

First, an example of horizontal inequity: Three taxpayers, all single, each using the standard deduction and one exemption, each making $12,000 a year, pay widely different taxes. A, who earns his $12,000 as an employee of General Motors, pays a tax of $1,952.50. B, an investor who made his $12,000 by selling off stock at a profit, pays $685.00 in tax. C, another investor, who received his $12,000 in interest on municipal bonds, paid no tax at all.

Second, an example of vertical inequity: Two men, each supporting a wife and two children on widely different salaries, both pay taxes at an effective rate of about 12 percent. Taxpayer A, whose $15,000 income was entirely due to salary, claiming personal exemptions and the standard deduction, paid $1,820 in taxes, or 12.1 percent of his total income. Taxpayer B had a total income of $40,000, composed of $5,000 of capital gains, $1,000 on dividends, and a $34,000 salary. He itemized his deductions, which included a payment on his new house, state income tax, property tax, interest on a loan he had made to buy stocks, and exclusion of $200 in dividends, and paid a tax of $4,892, or 12.2 percent of his total income.

The Internal Revenue Code's marginal tax rates, rising steeply from 14 to 70 percent of taxable income, create an illusion of greater progressivity than actually exists. Average effective tax rates show a different picture: rates rise progressively from 0.5 percent on incomes under $3,000 to 10.7 percent on incomes from $15,000 to $20,000. The rates plateau for incomes between $20,000 and $50,000, and increase to only 32.1 percent on millionaires.[14] In practice, therefore, our federal income tax is much less progressive than it appears.

Although primarily concerned here with reform of the income tax, I must note the effect of increasing payroll taxes on the equity and progressivity of the federal tax structure. While the income tax has been decreasing as a percent of total government receipts, payroll taxes have increased sharply. In 1964, the individual and corporate income tax brought in 64 percent of receipts, while social insurance taxes and contributions yielded only 19 percent. In 1974, the income tax is estimated to yield 58 percent of total receipts, and payroll taxes 30 percent.[15] The social security tax, by far the largest payroll deduction, is a levy at a flat percentage rate (5.85 percent) on the first $10,800 of wages. Thus a Milwaukee machinist making $10,000 a year now pays a payroll tax of 5.85 percent of his income, while the highly paid board chairman of a large corporation with an annual salary of $800,000 pays only .08 percent. And in 1971, according to the Treasury Department, 20 million workers too poor to pay any income taxes still had to pay $1.5 billion for social security.

Ideally, the services financed by these taxes should be funded from general revenues instead, and the payroll tax replaced by higher income tax rates. There is no reason why responsibility for society's elderly and handicapped should rest most heavily on the shoulders of low- and middle-income wage earners. Practically, however, the widespread attachment to the idea of social security as contributory retirement insurance would seem to preclude any such reform in the near future, though the financing of a portion of social security from general revenues may be possible. The regressivity of payroll taxes makes it all the more imperative to reform the income tax by eliminating tax loopholes which erode its progressivity.

Directions of Reform

The case for tax reform, then, rests on four points: the need for revenue, the need for jobs, the need for economic efficiency, and the need for equity. What specific tax reform would fulfill these requirements?

I foresee two stages of tax reform. The first stage would consist of immediate revenue-raising loophole-plugging reform, along the lines of my "quick-yield" bill, to help relieve the constraint so strikingly illustrated in the 1974 budget. Almost all of these provisions benefit wealthy taxpayers and large corporations exclusively. All of the provisions are familiar and have been the subject of recent debate in Congress. None requires further lengthy study. I regard passage of this bill, or of a similar measure, as a first priority for this Congress.

The second stage of tax reform should deal with the ticklish question of thorough structural reforms. I noted earlier that estimates of the revenue to be derived from tax reform vary greatly, depending on which loopholes are to be plugged. Pechman and Okner's $77 billion figure, for instance, assumes that homeowners' preferences would be eliminated, that transfer payments would be taxed as income, that charitable contributions and medical expenses would no longer be permitted as deductions. While it is aesthetically pleasing to contemplate a completely comprehensive tax base, as a matter of public policy, do we really want to eliminate these provisions—"loopholes" though they are—that do in fact provide substantial benefits to low- and middle-income taxpayers? What would be the revenue and distributive effects of doing so? Do we have something better to replace them with? There is very little hard evidence to answer these questions.

The attention of tax reformers has naturally been focused on wealthy tax avoiders and on the loopholes they use; as a result, much less is known about how personal exemptions and nonbusiness deductions affect the average taxpayer. More study and discussion of these provisions is needed before more sweeping tax reform is enacted.

Finally, what are the chances for tax reform this year? Can we expect strong leadership in this area from the White House? Based on the record, no. President Nixon's lack of enthusiasm for tax reform has been made abundantly clear. Not only has he consistently refused to send tax reform proposals to Congress when requested, but on such occasions as the April 1972 dinner at former Secretary of the Treasury

35

John Connally's ranch—when he told representatives of Texas's oil, industrial, and banking community that "I strongly favor not only the present depreciation rate, but going even further than that"—he has defended the oil depletion allowance. On February 6, 1973, Herbert Stein, the chairman of the Council of Economic Advisers, told Congress that the administration opposes using tax "reform" or "loophole-closing" to permit the continuance of programs omitted from the President's budget. Whatever tax reform proposals the Congress eventually obtains from the administration, they will not, said Mr. Stein, raise any revenue.[16]

But positive tax reform action by Congress is likely, for one reason. Congress, however slowly, reflects the will of the people, and the people want tax reform. A substantial share of this Congress was elected with a mandate for tax reform. If public pressure is maintained, this mandate will be carried out.

The news (based on preliminary figures) that 106 people with incomes over $200,000 paid no federal taxes in 1970, or that taxpayers caught by the new minimum tax paid at an average effective rate of 4 percent of preference income, is not in itself an analytical indictment of the tax system. In fact, the figures represent an improvement over the number of wealthy taxpayers escaping taxes in 1969. But such information brings home to the average American taxpayer the continuing inequity of our federal income tax. Similarly, figures showing that major oil companies paid an effective U.S. tax of only 6.7 percent on aggregate income exceeding $10 billion must bring home to less-privileged corporations,

36

which pay taxes at an average effective rate of 36 percent, that the system needs reform.

The American people's "taxpayers' revolt" was not appeased by the half-way reforms of the 1969 Tax Reform Act. As Dr. Charls E. Walker pointed out when he was then under secretary of the Treasury, the 1969 act is no more than a "highly important first step in reshaping the Federal tax system to make it fair and efficient." [17] Let us hope that 1973 gives the taxpayers of this country—both individuals and corporations—a long overdue second step.

REBUTTALS

CHARLS E. WALKER

Since I have only four minutes and have forty items on my list, I'm going to have to be selective. [Laughter.]

With respect to the 1969 act, I would like to quote an even greater American, Wilbur Mills, who said, after the act was passed, that this is a monumental effort at tax reform and the country should be proud of it. The statement of mine that Congressman Reuss quoted was made when we went to the Congress in April of '69, the first administration to move legislatively for tax reform in many years. We wanted to stage it over a two-to-three-year basis and not in one year. Also I was referring to the original approach and not the final act that passed. It was massive and monumental.

The congressman has asked the right questions. I'm not going to challenge him with respect to what we want our tax system to do. I would add points about the environment and social policy and other things you can do by subjecting people to a tax if they do the wrong thing and giving them a tax preference if they do the right thing.

Let's turn to the question of loopholes. You see what appear to be $70 million, $60 million, or $40 million of so-called loopholes, but when you really look into them, they aren't loopholes. Rather they're provisions that Congress enacted intentionally with the support of the people—like the deductibility of interest on the mortgage on your house, real estate taxes on your house, double exemptions for the blind over sixty-five, and so on. These aren't loopholes in my book and they're not loopholes in any particular congressman's book.

Mr. Reuss thinks that so-called loophole-closing will provide the additional revenue needed to support heavy increases in federal spending. But first, to correct a widespread misapprehension, the President's not cutting the budget. The budget's going up $18 billion this year over last and another $18 billion or $19 billion next year over this. It's the rate of increase that's slowing down.

Now, if you want to keep that rate of increase going up, the congressman says, let's reform taxes to raise revenues. Don't you believe it. I've lived through that. What tax reform means to the average, typical person is a reduction in his taxes. The Tax Reform Act of 1969, through the inexorable legislative process, turned into a massive tax cut. That was a very great disappointment to me personally. But once a tax bill gets out there on the floor, particularly of the Senate, boy, they cut taxes till you're blue in the face, because we've got a democracy and that's what people want. People don't like high taxes.

We have mentioned several so-called shelter areas, such as capital gains, the ADR system, hobby farms. Take hobby farms. If a person goes into the cattle-feeding business, he gets a tax preference now. The people want beef like crazy in this country and housewives are very unhappy about the price of beef going up. One way to get the price of beef down is to give more tax preferences for feeding cattle and getting choice beef in.

Each tax preference has its other side. I favor the oil depletion allowance if it is adjusted to force oil companies to plow back the benefits of depletion and intangible drilling costs into further explorations to help solve this energy crisis. If we don't do this, one day you're going to flip a switch in the East and the lights won't come on, because we'll be out of energy.

Mr. Reuss talked about Gulf Oil and the foreign tax credit. Gulf Oil pays huge taxes abroad. This is a difficult area. We need to do something about it, but it takes two to tango and you've got to tango with the sheiks in Kuwait and everybody else—[Laughter]—in order to work out this problem of the foreign tax credit.

As to income shares, using our tax system to redistribute income can be both fallacious and very pernicious if we destroy incentive in the process. And I will not accept a 125-year old quotation or forecast from Marx that has proved to be absolutely false—namely, that capitalism was driving to hell in a handbasket and very, very quickly. Mr. Marx was quite wrong on that score.

With respect to tax shelters, I very much favor a tightening of the minimum income tax. If the Congress had adopted the minimum income tax that the administration recommended in 1969, that list of wealthy nontaxpayers would be much smaller today. We sent up a tough one and it was very much watered down in the Congress.

I'll come back to the fundamental point. The real questions are these: Is our tax system biased against savings and investment and in favor of consumption? Shouldn't we take a hard look at this aspect of our tax system? I will raise this question for the question and answer period: Shouldn't we look at value-added taxes and other taxes on spending that would allow us to minimize the taxes on saving and investment—in order to get the economic growth and investment that we must have if we are to compete in an increasingly competitive world?

HENRY S. REUSS

Charlie Walker says that the American oil companies are merely tangoing with those sheiks over in the Middle East. Unfortunately, it's the American taxpayer, supporting a depletion allowance for foreign oil drilling as well as domestic, who pays for the music of that last tango. I think there ought to be an end to it.

Charlie says that we need beef in this country and so we ought to give the meat lobby even more of a tax preference than what they already have. Way last June I suggested to the administration a means of getting more beef in this country, namely, let the cattle into the 60 million acres of set-aside farmland, idled at the taxpayer's expense. The administration did nothing until last month, having said it couldn't be done. Finally it acted, but meanwhile the American housewife is paying 75 cents a pound for hamburger.

Charlie comes on strong for the investment tax credit as a great incentive to productivity and foreign trade earnings. If someone will design an investment tax credit that is really beamed at high-technology, export-oriented industries, I'll buy it. But the present one, which costs the taxpayers $3 billion a year, is for investment whether needed or unneeded, whether good, bad or outrageous.

Take the case of Mr. Joe Conforti, who owns a big chain of houses of prostitution in Nevada—where they're legal.

Joe was on television a few weeks ago bragging about how he just loves that 7 percent investment tax credit which he gets on new beds. [Laughter.] Says Joe: "I don't see any reason why my business shouldn't be treated just like any other business, and the Internal Revenue thinks the same way we do."

The American taxpayer thinks the whole thing is unfair and immoral and it wants those loopholes plugged.

I think this investment tax credit should be repealed. Business fixed investment in this country, according to the Council of Economic Advisers, is increasing this year over last at the rate of 14 percent. This added stimulus is just heaping fuel on the fires of inflation that exist anyway.

On this point, I'd like to quote from one of my favorite public figures: "Repeal of the investment credit will tend to dampen demand in a sector of the economy that is moving much too fast, the market for business equipment." That statement was made back in April 1969 at a time when business investment was rising at a rate of 10 percent as opposed to the 14 percent rate at which it's rising now, and the reasons for repealing the investment tax credit are much greater today than they were four years ago. The man who made that statement was, as I say, a great American, a great patriot and a great friend of mine, then Under Secretary of the Treasury Charlie Walker.

As I've said before, in 1969 Charlie Walker was my leader. It's just that in 1973 I think he's giving us some very poor advice.

DISCUSSION

THOMAS STANTON, Tax Reform Research Group: My question is for Mr. Walker. At a press conference on June 22, 1972, President Nixon promised he would send tax reform proposals to Congress by January 1, 1973. On June 24th Secretary of the Treasury Shultz wrote in a letter to Senator Javits that this statement by the President was "a firm commitment."

You were a very high official in the Treasury Department between June and the first of the year and I was wondering if you could tell us why the President was led to break his word?

DR. WALKER: I don't think the President has broken his word in the sense that he meant it in those press conferences and Secretary Shultz meant it. I think what he meant was that he would have proposals for the House Ways and Means Committee when Mr. Mills and his committee were really ready to take up tax reform, to receive the administration position.

Mr. Mills has elected to start the hearings with a series of panels to discuss the issues and then have public witnesses. As far as I know, and I have no inside information on this, the President will be sending tax proposals early in this session of Congress. If you want to make a federal case of January 1 versus, say, April 1, it's fine with me. I would simply say that the first major tax reform in the history of this republic was passed in the first year of a Republican administration and signed by a Republican President.

ROGER FREEMAN, Hoover Institution, Stanford University: My question is directed to Congressman Reuss. You refer to the huge tax loopholes which are available to rich people and enable them to escape their proper share of taxation. I wonder whether you have studied the amount of personal income which presently is not subject to the federal income tax. You may be, and I presume you are, aware of the fact that for 1970 out of $805 billion of personal income only about $400 billion was taxable, which means that about half of all personal income is not subject to taxation, federal taxation.

Have you studied the distribution of the $400 billion of nontaxed income between the high- and the low-income groups and have you come to any results?

MR. REUSS: Yes, I've made a study of it and I've relied particularly on the pioneering work of Pechman and Okner at Brookings Institution. From that work one concludes that, while, of course, great sums of income are remitted to taxpayers in the form of allowances for their children, medical expenses, home ownership costs and so on, all for perfectly equitable reasons, some $30 billion a year—underline that $30 *billion*—is excluded from adjusted gross income as a result of loopholes like the excluded half of capital gains, state and local bond interest, accelerated depreciation, percentage depletion.

The loopholes which add to the burden on the average taxpayer are in very large part precisely those loopholes which are enjoyed by wealthy tax avoiders who can employ the world's most skillful lawyers to point out these tax avoidance methods to them.

MR. FREEMAN: Do I understand then, congressman, that out of the $400 billion, about $30 billion accrue to high bracket taxpayers from capital gains and similar things and $370 billion to people in the middle, lower-middle and low-income groups, and that therefore you have about an 8 percent to 92 percent distribution of income not subject to taxation and almost all of it actually accrues to low, middle and low-income groups?

MR. REUSS: Yes. I may seem old-fashioned but to me $30 billion is a lot of money and if we could put just a small part of that—say, $10 billion—into the federal Treasury, then we could give tax relief to those who need it most—or at least freedom from the grinding succession of overall tax increases, which has been the lot of the average taxpayer, the average wage earner in this country.

So I say that, via loopholes, even $30 billion worth of income excluded from taxation is $30 billion too much. I say let us recapture at least part of that for the federal Treasury.

DR. WALKER: Let me comment on that. Under Secretary of the Treasury Edwin S. Cohen, who is recognized as one of the top tax experts in the United States, testified before the Joint Economic Committee last summer, of which Mr. Reuss is one of the senior distinguished members. Just to give you an idea of how the tax preferences hit various income groups, let's take several examples from his statement:

One, the deductibility of interest on mortgages on owner-occupied homes. That's no loophole to me; it's a loophole to some other people. The greatest benefit in this case was $719 million to people in the $10,000 to $15,000 income class.

Two, deductibility of property taxes on owner-occupied homes. The greatest benefit again was in that class.

Three, as far as the blind and the disabled and the aged, the greatest benefit was in the $7,000 to $10,000 class. And finally, for the net exclusion of pension contribution and earnings plans for employees, the greatest benefit was in the $10,000 to $15,000 class. These aren't the people who are having three martini lunches in Wall Street every week.

MR. REUSS: May I comment on the comment? I have these same figures and to me they tell a very different story. They tell me, and I'll document this, that the average wage earner, the average taxpayer, gets a crumb or two per tax-payer whereas the tax avoiders of great wealth clean up the lion's share.

Let's take the mortgage interest deduction. Moderate-income taxpayers—I'm not talking about poverty cases but about people with an income of $10,000 to $15,000 a year—get an average of $50.97 benefits per capita from this provision, whereas wealthy people—those with incomes of $100,000 and up—get $410.78 per capita.

Or take the medical deduction. The middle-income tax-payer gets $33.00 per capita, wealthier people $449.00. Or the treatment of capital gains, from which middle-income people get $16.31 in benefits, wealthy people $38,000.

DR. WALKER: You can't compare these figures.

MR. REUSS: Of course there are more lower and average income people in this country and of course if you add the figures for them together it makes a nice sum. But the fact is that these loopholes and preferences benefit largely the very wealthy, and that's what's wrong with them.

DR. WALKER: This is exactly the point. In a progressive income tax system, the higher your income the more you benefit from a deduction. Now you don't want to get rid of the progressive income tax system, do you? That's the way to reduce the benefit for those guys.

ROBERT GALLAMORE, Common Cause: Dr. Walker, you stated that you believed our present tax system created a bias against investment. It seems to me that several of the tax loopholes we've talked about this evening are in fact a double subsidy of investments. One example is percentage depletion for oil companies and favorable capital gains treatment for stockholders. Another example is the investment tax credit coupled with the new ADR system. Another is export subsidies coupled with the domestic sales corporation or DISC.

It seems to me that these provisions in fact are very favorable to investment and run counter to the interests of the general taxpayer.

DR. WALKER: There are several comments I could make to that question which would have to do with the foreign tax credit and the investment tax credit, and I would have commented on Mr. Reuss's earlier presentation, if there had been time.

There is a bill before the Congress today called the Burke-Hartke bill which would eliminate both the deferral of the foreign tax and the foreign tax credit. What you've got to understand is that the multinational corporation that this proposal would hit is simply a corporation domiciled in the United States. Change its tax treatment along the lines of this proposal and it will become domiciled elsewhere. The federal government won't get any revenue out of that.

But the point I really want to make is this. Beginning under the leadership of John Kennedy in 1961-62 and with the good help of Walter Heller and Douglas Dillon and Joe Fowler, we started moving towards reducing tax rates on investments. We have made progress but we haven't gone far enough. I'll conclude with one example.

What got the investment credit and the accelerated depreciation through the Congress in 1971 was one simple table, one piece of paper which I hold in my hand. It compares the cost to businessmen here and abroad of buying new productive equipment, allowing for the corporate tax, tax allowances, tax credits and the depreciation system. In 1970 the equipment which cost the businessman in the United States 100 cents, cost the businessman in Japan and most Western European countries 79 to 83 cents. The Revenue Act of 1971 lowered the cost to the American businessman to about 87 cents, which is still quite a bit higher than what foreign businessmen are paying. And this is at a time when we've got a $6 billion trade deficit—and don't think that isn't a major problem. It is a horrendous problem.

MR. REUSS: I must respond briefly to the suggestion by Dr. Walker that if we tax multinationals on the same basis as we do American corporations—that is, make them pay an income tax on their income whether they pay it out in dividends or not—that somehow they're going to desert the United States and hightail it for overseas. I have just two

54

comments on that. First, when they do that, they may soon find that things aren't so glorious in Bulgaria or Bangladesh or wherever they go to. Second, however, I would favor a charitable—indeed, a liberal—attitude toward them and would be glad to give them amnesty if they wanted to come back. [Laughter.]

GERARD BRANNON, Georgetown University: Dr. Walker, I was interested in your comment that the oil depletion allowance should be limited to companies that reinvest in oil drilling. Doesn't this highlight the defect of specialized tax incentives? In effect you want to say that there should be subsidy for investment in oil drillings but this should be limited to companies who got their money from oil in the first place through the oil depletion allowance.

If you want to subsidize oil investment, wouldn't it be better to do it outright and not limit it to companies that earn their money from oil?

DR. WALKER: Two comments. By the way, that is my very good friend and former helper in the Treasury Department, Gerry Brannon, who is a tower of strength on the investment credit—not on depletion but on the investment credit. [Laughter.]

Some of my former bosses at Treasury disagree very strongly with this, but if you give me a choice of achieving a good social goal through a tax action on the one hand or an outright government subsidy on the other hand, I'll take the tax approach every time—for two reasons. One, it works through the market process and induces the company (or person) to do something it wouldn't do if it weren't for the tax subsidy. Second, you do not have to create a federal bureaucracy to administer the subsidy on the basis of the judgment of certain individuals, however well meaning, in various departments.

Now with respect to the depletion and the plow-back proposal, which I've been supporting for some time. As Woodrow Wilson said when the Federal Reserve System was set up, we don't have a clean sheet of paper to work on, we are not remaking the economy anew from the word go.

Today we have an oil depletion allowance of 22 percent. It originated from a compromise between the House and Senate in the 1920s on the basis of what each thought was actual depletion. One house said 30 percent, the other 25 percent and, in our great system, 27½ was the result. Then in the 1969 act it was reduced to 22 percent. Maybe you can get it repealed and put in this direct subsidy instead; but I would rather take what we have and work with it in the political process to make it a better way to help solve the energy crisis—which it can be with plow back.

GEORGE WILL, *National Review*: I have a question related to the use of subsidies and tax incentives. Both debaters agree that the tax system should be used to encourage a proper balance between consumption and investment. They differ as to whether we've hit that proper balance.

My question is whether or not both may not be giving the government the unwarranted benefit of altogether warranted doubts as to its ability to fine tune the economy with the revenue system. Given the limited data we have available, given the legislative lag that may be up to two years in tampering with the tax system, is this really an efficient way to regulate these matters?

MR. REUSS: A good question. I would agree with the implication of the questioner. I think the tax system is not a very good way to fine tune the economy and that we would do best if we attempted to shoot at full employment without inflation in this country and let investment, for instance, adopt a harmonious posture with respect to what consumers, in a full-employment economy, want to take off the market. I think that's a much better approach than hypo-ing investment by these various devices.

DR. WALKER: I think we're talking about two different things here. As far as using the tax system for fine tuning in a macroeconomic sense—in other words, for affecting total problems of inflation and supply and demand in the economy —I am very much against that. I think it disrupts business planning. I think the idea that we should turn the investment credit on and off, either at the will of Congress or the President, is a very bad idea, even though my old friend Arthur Burns has been endorsing it recently.

I'm talking about something different. I'm talking about using tax preferences or tax penalties to promote social goals. Let me give you just three examples of this approach that the Nixon administration was able to get into the 1969 act: We got a five-year fast write-off amortization for rehabilitating low-income housing. We got a five-year fast write-off for railroad car rolling stock because, if you remember in 1969, wheat was rotting out in the West due to an absence of railroad freight cars. And we got a five-year fast write-off for investment in antipollution equipment.

These provisions expire in five years unless the Congress finds reasons to extend them. To me they represent the best of all worlds in the use of tax preferences for social goals. And the purpose is not fine tuning. It's to achieve social goals rather than economic growth and stability.

NORMAN TURE, Norman B. Ture Incorporated: Mr. Walker—if I may take the liberty of elaborating by asking a question—it seemed to me that in your remarks concerning the disparity in the weight of taxation on saving and investment on the one hand and consumption on the other, you were talking about something more than merely the seeking out of particular objectives of social policy.

It seemed to me that you were addressing yourself to the point that, analytically, it can be shown very simply that our present income tax structure and other features of our overall tax system impose a much, much more substantial cost for buying future income—that is, for saving, and, therefore, for investing—than they do for equal amounts of consumption. Against a standard of equal treatment of saving and consumption, many of the things that are called loopholes do not appear to be loopholes at all. They represent only very modest abatements of that bias. Certainly the tax on capital gains cannot be regarded as a loophole. It ought to be regarded as an additional penalty tax on saving and investing.

DR. WALKER: I can't find much in that to disagree with. [Laughter.]

You know, I'll bet it's going to surprise many of you people out there in television-land to hear that the United States taxes capital gains more heavily than almost any other country in the world. Now you can ask yourself a question. Do all those people in all those other countries, some of which have been growing rapidly—galloping, relative to us—have their heads screwed on wrong?

Maybe they've got something with this value-added tax. I hate to open up a completely new issue but it's involved here. For example, you make x thousand dollars a year, I make x thousand dollars a year. Let's assume you and I make the same amount. Now in terms of the income tax, given the same deductions and same family situation and so forth, you and I will pay the same basic federal tax. But let's suppose that you're a very thrifty person and you save a big part of your income and put it in a savings and loan to build houses and you put it into bonds to build factories and you put it into the savings investment process and, as a result, we get a lot of good economic growth and jobs. But suppose I throw my income away on wine, women and song and high living and don't save a bit.

Under the income tax system we both pay the same rate but under a value-added tax system—which is not really a sales tax, it is a spending tax—the person that spends and doesn't save pays a higher rate. It's time we started thinking about that. These Europeans that are going in that direction are not all that dumb.

MR. REUSS: Before commenting on that point, let me first respond briefly to Mr. Ture's question about whether we have enough incentive for business investment. Wasn't that your question?

MR. TURE: No, Congressman Reuss, I was not talking about incentives at all. I don't regard these provisions as incentives. I regard them as extremely mild abatements of enormous bias against saving and investment.

59

MR. REUSS: All right. You say there's a bias against saving and investment. I point out that savings in this country have been enormous. Some $70 billion or $80 billion has trickled over to Europe in the Eurodollar market. Incentives are the greatest ever, corporate profits the greatest in the history of the republic. So don't tell me that we don't offer sufficient inducements to save and to invest.

Now as to the value-added tax, let me just say that it isn't going to help very much for the average wage earner to be told that things are a little better for him, if, as a result of things being improved a bit, he has a sales tax called a value-added tax piled onto him. I had thought that the value-added tax had been laid to rest by the recent studies of the very nonpartisan Advisory Commission on Intergovernmental Relations. Apparently it is an idea that is still being toyed with by the administration.

I persist in saying that if we need more income in the federal Treasury, which we do, the way to get it is by a progressive tax rather than by another sales tax.

DR. WALKER: I've got to make one comment on that. I very much agreed with the point in Congressman Reuss's paper to the effect that we should be very, very concerned about the great growth in the payroll tax in this country. So I would like to suggest consideration of a value-added tax—which can be put on a nonregressive basis very easily and made proportional—for, say, $25 billion to use to substitute completely for the payroll tax.

MR. REUSS: I think the answer of the American wage earner, if he ever understood that, would be to say, Thank you, Mr. Walker, for wanting to reduce our payroll tax, which is miserable, but thanks for nothing: you only offer to put another sales tax on middle-income people. That's what it would do, even with a little relief for the very poor.

DR. WALKER: Then you have to ask yourself, why did the workers and the unions support the value-added tax in Scandinavia? There is a very simple reason why they did and why I predict that, one, we will have a value-added tax in this country within six to eight years and, two, the liberal establishment will be supporting it in two to four years. The reason is that it is one hell of a revenue raiser and, if we want to support the level of spending that the liberal establishment wants to support, the best tax to support it is the value-added tax and not a progressive income tax that drives every taxpayer of any bracket up the wall every April 15th.

MR. REUSS: I'm glad I don't belong to that liberal establishment. [Laughter.]

DR. WALKER: You're free to continue to oppose the value-added tax.

PAUL McCRACKEN, University of Michigan: One aspect of tax policy has to do with fiscal policy, that is, using our budgetary process for stabilization purposes. I noticed the economic report contained some cautiously sympathetic comments in regard to giving the President some limited authority to vary tax rates. Would the two participants please comment on this aspect of the tax policy?

DR. WALKER: I'm against it. I'm against it and, as Dr. McCracken knows, I'm an economist by training and a sort of political observer by experience. I realize some safeguards could be worked in to such an arrangement. Congressman Reuss may have had some. I know Congressman

61

Moorhead has suggested safeguards. But in our political democracy to give the President, any President, a power which he might use in October of a year divisible by four in sort of a positive direction, that bothers me.

I think that if we would stabilize the whole fiscal picture within a full-employment budget balance concept, then basically monetary policy is the tool for variation in the short run, not fiscal policy.

MR. REUSS: This is ridiculous. Dr. Walker, a loyal Republican, opposes the President's suggestion and I, a contentious Democrat, am fairly sympathetic to it. I think, with proper safeguards—which Charlie Walker is fair enough to say have been suggested—the tax rates should be modestly variable to take account of the business cycle. I think both monetary policy and fiscal policy ought to have a little more flexibility than they've had.

DR. WALKER: One other point on that—and I'm not really contesting with the congressman here. Economic analysis undertaken in the Department of the Treasury and elsewhere very strongly supports—I don't want to get deep into economic theory—what is called the Friedman permanent income hypothesis. According to that hypothesis, if you temporarily raise or lower taxes people don't pay much attention to it because they look beyond it. We saw this in the case of withholding recently and we're going to see it this year and we saw it in the case of the 1968 tax surcharges. The 1968 tax increase didn't seem to have much bang because people thought it would expire.

DAVE O'NEILL, American Enterprise Institute: I'd like to address a general question to both speakers. On the one hand, Charlie Walker seems to be saying that there's an important trade-off between making the tax system more progressive and economic growth—forgetting for a minute now about stability—and, on the other, Congressman Reuss seems to be saying that we can make the tax system more progressive without losing much in terms of economic growth. Is there any objective evidence that either of you can cite as to where we are in this trade-off point and as to whether we wouldn't seriously lower the growth rate by, say, a tenth of a percentage point, if we went in your direction. As you know, people like Ed Dennison have shown that a tenth of a percentage point over twenty years can really, seriously, affect the nation's economic well-being?

MR. REUSS: Yes, I think there's some evidence supporting the Democratic party's idea that the nation prospers best when consumer income and spending power are most widely spread and that businessmen in that kind of an economy will have the best possible incentive to invest: namely, the opportunity to sell the products that their expanded factories can make. We had some evidence of this in 1963, '64 and '65, when great progress toward full employment without inflation was made—before we got into the disastrous Vietnam War.

The evidence is not all in but, by and large, I think that the percolate-up theory is better than the trickle-down. Trickle-down means that you give tax and other benefits to corporations in the hope that they will invest and somehow this will make jobs in some way never quite clear to me.

MODERATOR GORALSKI: Are you a percolater-upper or a tricklator-downer?

DR. WALKER: I'm sort of in between. Half my friends are for this and half my friends are for that, and I never disagree with my friends. [Laughter.]

I've been away too long from the disciplines of the profession to be able to cite specific evidence. But I do remember a meeting of Treasury Department consultants not too long ago where Professor Robert Mundell, a very distinguished economist from the University of Chicago, argued persuasively that the tax system in Japan, which is less burdensome on these things we're talking about than our own, was in his judgment providing a very good demonstration of the relationship between economic growth and keeping the burden on saving and investment down. This is the sort of thing that one cannot and should not answer with a seat-of-the-pants opinion. We need a lot more work and a lot more cross-fertilization between the conservative think tanks and the liberal think tanks. We need sort of a truce so that we can sit down and determine the answers. I've faith that the scholars, and I know them and like them, will get to the answers.

DAVID MEISELMAN, Virginia Polytechnic Institute: Congressman Reuss, in your paper you have some comments on the asset depreciation range system and the investment tax credit and you contend that the recent rise in the rate of capital formation will tend to cost jobs. Somehow you give us the impression in that discussion that, rather than stimulate a frenzy of uneconomic investment, et cetera, we should aim for a slow and maintained increase in investment. This suggests to me that you believe that somehow if we have less capital formation, we will have more jobs and perhaps have a higher level of income.

Do you really believe that? Would you extend that perhaps to slowing down the rate of investment as a means for increasing employment?

MR. REUSS: Certainly not. And I am glad to have the chance to make clear that I am not a Luddite, a fellow who wants to throw a wooden shoe in the machinery. I think that our government has an obligation under the Employment Act of 1946 to do everything possible to provide full employment without inflation.

Now, let's be clear about capital investment. Capital investment is a good thing. It does increase productivity. At the time the new machines are being made, it even creates extra jobs while men make those machines. But later on, if too many machines have been made and if you slow down, then not only don't those workers make machines any more, but the men who use the machines find that they have fewer customers to place orders which they have to fulfill.

Therefore, what we need to do in this country is, first, to keep a rather steady level of capital investment, to avoid these artificial shots of adrenalin every now and then which tend, because we overbuild, to make a boom and bust economy.

Second, it is the obligation of the government to recognize that machines do put men out of work. That is part of their necessary result. Therefore the government has to see to it that, overall, there are enough jobs so that everybody able and willing to work has a chance at a job. And we are not doing that now. I say that we want to get off the kick of spending $6 billion a year—as we now are—in stimulating unnecessary investment now that should take place in the future and use part of that recovered money in a public service job program to put some of the less skilled unemployed to work.

DR. WALKER: I have got to challenge strongly certain points of the congressman's answer to Mr. Meiselman.

I don't mean to be facetious when I say that if one carries this argument all the way back, that fellow Watt did a great disservice in inventing the steam engine. Look at all the horses he put out of work, not to mention the people. However we don't have to go back that far. Remember the late 1950s when the Cassandras were saying the computer age would throw people out of work like crazy? Today you can't watch TV—I'm a Channel 5 fan in this city because it has the old movies of the '40s [Laughter]—and the only thing wrong with watching "The Maltese Falcon" is that every other five minutes there's an ad for a computer school where you can go and learn something that'll get you a job and make you a lot of money.

This ties in with Dr. O'Neill's question. I think it can probably be demonstrated—I'm not sure it has yet—that the investment tax credit and accelerated depreciation tend more to stimulate the investment in better equipment and modernized equipment. But when there's a boom rolling along like we have now, the generated demand—the accelerator that the economists talk about—will take over and push you along. But the investment credit raises the rate of return to businessmen after taxes and entices them to try to build steel mills as modern as the steel mills in Japan. And,

66

believe me, we've only got one or two that compare with the Japanese mills.

And that is what the shouting is all about. If we don't modernize we'll have to draw a ring around this country and live all by ourselves. But we can't do that if we are going to have the kind of open world that both you and I want, Henry.

MR. REUSS: One additional comment: this trickle-down theory, the rapid depreciation, investment credit, feed-the-horses-so-the-sparrows-will-thrive theory, has resulted in unemployment going up over the last four years from 3.3 percent to 5 percent and higher. I think we have a job to make useful work for everyone willing and able to work in this country, and the trickle-down theory by itself simply doesn't do it. So I won't accept the idea that just by giving a shot in the arm to capital investment we can have done with the job of getting full employment without inflation.

DR. WALKER: So you're saying the capital boom of the late 1960s reflected the investment credit, et cetera. My judgment is—

MR. REUSS: Reflected the war.

DR. WALKER: Exactly. If we didn't want the great investment boom of the late 1960s, we should not have superimposed a war costing $30 billion a year—

MR. REUSS: Amen.

DR. WALKER: —on top of a full-employment economy.

MR. REUSS: Amen.

DR. WALKER: So the villain—

MR. REUSS: How I agree with you!

DR. WALKER: so the villain was the war and not the investment tax credit. That's my point.

MR. REUSS: The villain *was* the war. Since we don't have that kind of a war today, thank God, the villain now is largely these hyperthyroid investment incentives.

DR. WALKER: Are you saying that we've got too much demand now and we ought to pull back—that we don't have slack that ought to be taken up?

MR. REUSS: That is precisely what I am saying. I am saying that in heavy industry, in shipbuilding, in armaments, et cetera, by reason of government spending and government tax bonanzas, a boiling inflation is now starting. On the other hand, we have 4.5 million people with very simple skills who don't fit into the job slots for skilled labor provided by the expansion of heavy industry.

My answer is to stop the inflation in the heavy industry sector where the government started it and put some of the savings into making jobs for the people who desperately need jobs. We will have a better balanced country. The administration is always talking about balance. Why not start right there?

DR. WALKER: Well, I'm not sure you can demonstrate that a dollar spent for capital investment causes more inflation than a dollar spent for a government program which is a manifest failure. [Laughter.] In fact, I think it's the other way around. So I will take the President's approach of holding the budget to a quarter of a trillion dollars as the basic bastion in the battle against inflation.

TOM STANTON, Tax Reform Research Group: I would like to ask both participants: The Revenue Act of 1971 included a very expensive subsidy which we would call the investment credit. The Nixon administration presented it to the American people in the name of the job development tax credit. For the billions of dollars that this subsidy cost, how many jobs did that credit develop last year?

DR. WALKER: I don't have precise figures, but it created a lot of jobs—particularly if you look not just at people working, but also at increased overtime and the increased workweek. We can't go through all the figures here.

But, you see, you're arguing with Mr. Reuss. He is saying that the investment credit is doing too much to stimulate the economy, and I'm saying that it is a good thing. And a big portion of that increase in jobs absorbed a very rapid labor force increase. We have reduced unemployment down to about 5 percent. I think that the reenactment of the job development credit is the best thing since home cooking.

MR. REUSS: The investment tax credit certainly didn't increase jobs for the 42-year-old janitor in Chicago—black, making $7,000 a year—whose job was shampooing the floor of the office building in which he worked. As a result of the investment tax credit, his employer bought an automatic shampooer. The janitor lost his job and he is now on welfare in Chicago, all as reported by one of the leading business magazines.

Again, I don't want to throw an automatic shampooer into the machine, but I think that if we take jobs from people by increasing the use of machinery, it is up to the government and the people of the United States to provide useful jobs for these unemployed, not to throw them on the welfare slag heap.

DR. WALKER: I was trying to think of a 90-year-old I could counter with—[Laughter]—who got a job.

MR. WILL: We frequently hear it said that we are reaching the point at which the public sector is absorbing the upper limit of the gross national product that it can absorb without stifling the energies of the country. I would like to hear both debaters' opinions on this subject. Are we really reaching that limit? Second, is the percent of the GNP a reliable index of this problem? And, third, what do you look for in terms of evidence that a society is becoming enervated in some way by excessive growth of the public sector?

MR. REUSS: I think comparative figures show that the United States tax burden—state, federal, local—is appreciably less than that of most major European countries. There are some exceptions. But ours is around 33 percent of total income. The burden in most European countries hovers up around 40 percent.

Having said that, however, I am not joyous about increasing the overall tax rate in this country. I think there are many areas—state, local, federal—where we could cut down by cutting out waste and unnecessary things. I applaud President Nixon's cutting out funds for the Subversive Activities Control Board, and for impacted school aid—saving a nickel here and a million there. That's fine. The more of that we can do, the better.

But when you ask whether the American public is enervated by the amount of government spending, my observation is that the American public wants government funds spent on worthy projects—education, health, the environment. What is having an enervating effect, and quite understandably, is a tax system so full of loopholes that it looks like a Swiss cheese. That is why enervation occurs.

DR. WALKER: Yes. The answer in my judgment, Mr. Will, is a political answer, or a politico-economic answer, and not really an economic answer.

A well-known economist from Down Under said some quarter of a century ago that if total taxes get above 25 percent of GNP, you're going to go to hell in a handbasket. Demonstrably this was not true. In periods of national emergency and national patriotism, we quite obviously will bear a much larger tax burden. And our relative tax burden probably is not as high as it is in many other countries.

But I think the real issue here is that—and, believe me, from working closely with the Congress for fourteen years and with various committees in the Congress, I have come to a conclusion that surprises my son who is a junior in college—we've got a democracy. We really do—and it works. I mean the public will get through to the Congress and things happen. Sometimes it takes time. Sometimes things happen too quickly when you have an emotional surge that kills an SST or something like that.

When I go around the country, I talk to everybody I can. I talk to cabdrivers, bellhops, and elevator operators (where they are not automated) and I talk to presidents of corporations and banks and to people in between. I found during the last year that the American people had had it up to here—not with government in general, but they were convinced they were not getting enough bang from the bucks they were sending to Washington.

So as a politico-economic phenomenon, we are at or above the limit in one sense of the term—until some event occurs that changes people's attitudes and causes the limit to move up or down to another plateau. The President knows this. The people know this. The Congress knows this. And that in my judgment is why the battle of the budget, 1973, was over before it started.

DR. TURE: Congressman Reuss, you made some observations in your prepared statement concerning the changes in the distribution of income in the United States. I am curious about the source of that information. I have just completed a study in which I had occasion to consult Census Bureau data pertaining to income distribution, both pre- and post-tax, and I checked these distributions out for every year from 1947 through 1968.

If you draw the curves that represent those income distributions, you will find that virtually all of them fall one on top of the other. The amount of the spread between them is very small, and the difference from year to year is utterly random. It seems to me to be nothing but statistical noise.

So I am very curious as to what the source of these conflicting data that you remarked on is.

MR. REUSS: My source, Dr. Ture, was the Bureau of the Census, *Consumer Income: Money Income in 1971 of Families and Persons in the United States,* published two months ago. It showed, for example, that the wealthiest 20 percent of the American families increased their share of the national income a full percentage point just in the three-year period 1968-71.

Even, however, if the Bureau of the Census is wrong and those figures are fabricated by some internal saboteur, which I don't think they are, there still are approximately 8,000 reasons why we ought to plug tax loopholes.

DR. TURE: Congressman Reuss, may I offer a gratuitous suggestion—that you ask a member of your staff actually to take that Census Bureau data, which are the same data that I used, and to plot them for each year on transparencies and lay the one on top of the other and see how many years in which you can find a difference discernible by the naked eye without the aid of an electronic microscope.

MR. REUSS: I'll be delighted. [Laughter.]

MODERATOR GORALSKI: Thank you both very, very much for a very stimulating discussion of our rational debate topic, Major Tax Reform—Urgent Necessity or Not?

NOTES

NOTES TO SECOND LECTURE

[1] Percentages for years prior to 1973 from Charles L. Schultze, et al., *Setting National Priorities, The 1973 Budget* (Washington, D.C.: The Brookings Institution, 1972), pp. 398-403. Percentages for 1973 calculated from *The Budget of the United States Government, Fiscal Year 1974* (Washington, D.C.: U.S. Government Printing Office, 1973).

[2] Schultze, et al., *Setting National Priorities,* p. 411.

[3] David J. Ott, et al., *Nixon, McGovern and the Federal Budget* (Washington, D.C.: American Enterprise Institute, 1972), pp. 6-7.

[4] *The Budget,* 1974, p. 46.

[5] See respectively, *The Economics of Federal Subsidy Programs,* A Staff Study Prepared for the Use of the Joint Economic Committee, 92nd Congress, 1st session, January 11, 1972, p. 31; and Joseph A. Pechman and Benjamin A. Okner, "Individual Income Tax Erosion by Income Classes," in *The Economics of Federal Subsidy Programs,* A Compendium of Papers Prepared for the Use of the Joint Economic Committee, 92nd Congress, 2nd session, part 3, 1972.

[6] Statement by Stanley S. Surrey before Committee on Ways and Means, U.S. House of Representatives, February 5, 1973.

[7] Peggy B. Musgrave, "Tax Preferences to Foreign Investment," *The Economics of Federal Subsidy Programs,* A Compendium, part 2, p. 194.

[8] *Economic Report of the President, 1973* (Washington, D.C.: U.S. Government Printing Office, 1973), pp. 19 and 83.

[9] U.S., Bureau of the Census, *Consumer Income: Money Income in 1971 of Families and Persons in the United States* (Washington, D.C.: U.S. Government Printing Office, 1972). All the above income distribution statistics are contained in Table 14 of that publication except the 1971 figure for the top 5 percent, which was supplied at my request by a Census Bureau official.

[10] Karl Marx, *Capital,* vol. I (Moscow: Progress Publishers, 1965), pp. 625-640.

[11] U.S., Department of the Treasury, Internal Revenue Service, *Preliminary Statistics of Income 1970: Individual Income Tax Returns* (Washington, D.C.: U.S. Government Printing Office, 1972), p. 29.

[12] U.S., Congress, House Committee on Ways and Means and Senate Committee on Finance, *Tax Reform Studies and Proposals U.S. Treasury Department* (1969) part 4, for these and following figures. Edward W. Erickson and Stephen W. Millsaps, "Taxes, Goals, and Efficiency: Petroleum and Defense," *The Economics of Federal Subsidy Programs,* A Compendium, part 3, pp. 286-303, update this analysis to include effects of the 1969 depletion reduction. They criticize the specific figures of the Treasury report, but agree with their conclusion.

[13] Statistics provided at my request by the Independent Petroleum Association of America.

[14] Joseph A. Pechman and Benjamin A. Okner, *Individual Income Tax Erosion by Income Classes* (Washington, D.C.: The Brookings Institution, 1972), p. 22. These rates are calculated for expanded adjusted gross income, not taxable income.

[15] Calculated from *The Budget,* 1974, Table 16, pp. 362-363.

[16] *New York Times,* November 30, 1972, p. 23.

[17] Statement of Charls E. Walker, Under Secretary of the Treasury, before the House Ways and Means Committee, April 22, 1969.